Crescent Beach Reflections

Author: Ben Nuttall-Smith
                www.bennuttall-smith.ca

Publisher: Rutherford Press
                www.rutherfordpress.ca
For information, contact:

                Rutherford Press,
                Richmond, BC, Canada
                info@rutherfordpress.ca
                www.rutherfordpress.ca

Printed in the United States of America and Canada

ISBN (paperback) # 978-1-988739-04-5

ISBN (ebook)   # 978-1-988739-05-2

Illustrations by Ben Nuttall-Smith

Book design by George Opacic

CRESCENT BEACH REFLECTIONS

poetry

ben nuttall-smith

Rutherford Press

I N D E X

Poetry and Reading

D E D I C A T I O N

To my soulmate,

muse and

partner in many

of these poems

– Margot Thomson

artists in residence

HOME

&

NATURE

Crescent Beach Reflections

Great expanse of mud and sand,

a rocky bank and water birds,

joggers in the rain.

9

Brown ever turns to brilliant gold,

when sunshine dapples through the clouds,

to paint the trees with silver lace

and sparkle on the bay.

A stately conference of Heron

debate the gulls about the evening catch

and call the tide to shore.

Above the mottled pools, a pair of eagles glide

while crows protest the rumbly train

that groans and grinds its way

around the headland to the bay.

In early May, the children flock like ducklings,

with buckets, spades, boots and yellow hats.

They squat in puddles, tease the crabs,

and dig for oceans in the watery sand.

Along the shore, their minders sit on logs.

While they watch, they chatter, drink their tea,

and call in vain to stragglers in the pools.

As far as eye can see, paddlers wander out

on miles and miles of sand and weed,

through shallow pools, all shimmering
beneath the morning glare.
Gulls, white, brown, grey, squabble
at a hamper in the sand,
while wrappers gaily flutter in the wind.

A dozen kites swim hard against the breeze,
like minnows with long waggling tails.
One swoops to chase a crow;
and then its crosspiece snaps,
to meet stern justice on the rocks below.
Despite the angry stones hurled at its taunts
crow flaps down to strut and sound rebuke.

Blankets, chairs, umbrella, hamper, radio,
another gang of picnickers arrives by car,
to taste a summer day at Crescent Beach.
Through steamy miles of traffic horns
and roaring trucks, they've traveled far,
to sit upon the sand
and blare their choice of joy for all to share.

Summer Storm

summer storm strikes.
tumbling,
sky-black giants trespass.
soggy sun slips out of sight.
cymbals clash,
heavens' floodgates open.
rain pummels the pond.
lily pods hunker down tight on the water.
swallow dips
under crown of rose bush.
safe and secure
beneath her majesty.
shaken rose,
drips pink teardrops.
sky-black giants dissolve.
soggy sun emerges triumphant.
summer storm subsides.

God Smiles

Morning after big storm

skies celestial blue

sun sparkles

icicle-decked branches

heavily laden

refined sugar

crocuses

bravely peer

from beneath

eiderdown

see

it's safe to rejoice

God smiles

Deer in my Garden

down in the garden, on all fours,
i'm pulling weeds; a frequent chore
when summer sun is not too high.
suddenly, i chance to spy
a pair of hoofs and legs, and then
another two, the very same.

"hello!" say i, "and what's your name?
not Bambi surely, standing, lunching,
unperturbed, 'midst roses, munching.

slowly i rise, not to fright.
a deer in my garden, what delight!
a sudden movement from behind;
i turn to face another friend,
Bambi's brother, standing tall.
my raspberries! "don't eat them all."
and then, beneath the apple tree,
with antlers great, stands number three,
chewing at leaves contentedly.

"if you will kindly stay right there,
i'll fetch my camera, so's to share,
how privileged i am to stand
with nature's creatures close at hand."

Morning on a Country Road

Vancouver Island, Spring 1951

The frogs on the riverbank grow silent.

Stars low on the western horizon yield

to early morning light.

Rising sun splashes the crest of the hill with scarlet,

breakfast greeting for a new day.

A light breeze rustles in the trees.

Plants shed their night dew,

reach for sun's morning blessing.

Puffy clouds trail lambs' tails,

patchy streamers, edges tinted pink.

Mists billow up the lake.

Flocks of ducks and geese

circle in clamorous flight to bed on open water.

From low bushes a flock of grouse explode into flight.

Crows circle and dive in delight,

cawing advice to early travellers.

Kamikaze eagle protects her nest.

A turquoise dragonfly loiters then lands

on a black rock to stretch iridescent wings.

Owl, perched on an overhanging limb,

stares grave and silent.

First tender leaves of arbutus glisten

bright green against oxblood trunk and limbs.

The air is filled with cries and noise of restless spirits.

Deep in the forest, light oozes through ancient oaks.

A pair of horned owls speak to one another.

A rodent shrieks, soon to be fed to a nest of ravenous owlets.

Old Raccoon attempts to climb metal pole to reach birdseed.

He jumps and scratches valiantly at the slippery metal,

topples back time and again.

Exhausted, he toddles off in search of scraps between the huts.

Tonight he'll be back to try again.

You Don't Know Snow

You don't know snow
until you've heard coyotes howl;
your eyes and whiskers frosted shut
and from your nether regions, feeling gone.
If hell is real, there'll be no fire
just icy winds across a barren plain.
You don't know snow
until the saw-edged bite of frost
burns your numbed toes and fingertips
when they're forced awake.

Penny's Garden

A wild garden grows

by a cottage near the bay.

The trellis is old and faded

but beauty still climbs her frame,

and crowns the posts

where the garden gate was hung.

Thick moss beneath the cypress tree

stretches onto the old rope swing.

Periwinkle scatters on the garden path

where Thrushes still warble and sing.

The clematis reaches tall

to the bickering blackbirds

protesting the mere presence

of an old yellow cat

perched on the great stone wall.

This is Penny's garden,

and perhaps it's known better days

but old memories survive and come alive

when I walk that Periwinkle path

at dusk with Penny's ghost.

Evening Sounds

Music leaves her notes among the roses
every flower that blossoms deposits a tone
in pentatonic harmony with the evening breeze.
Moon sings her silent song to attending stars.

Foothills Country

B.C. Interior, May 2015

Rusted cars and burned out oil barrels
insult the pastoral countryside,
incongruous beneath snow-dusted pines
along this windy road.

Here, beside a log-strewn stream,
tree carcasses surround an abandoned
once-white trailer,
sagging in the swamp grass.
Sentry maple leaf flag hangs limp

Nature's Lament

Clouds drape the darkening face of evening.

Air hangs heavy with tears that cannot fall

the world holds her breath

for an unnamed lament

heard only by the stones.

With the first slap of thunder,

birds retreat and melt forever

into the forest beyond the crag,

leaving an ocean vista flushed and bare

before the sinking orb.

In the deluge, drunken berries float in puddles

along the pebbly path.

Petals on the water

make their way in streams.

Rivers carry secrets to the sea.

A Walk in the Woods in October

Nature nudges the season's breast,

into a million subtle hues,

spreading her technicolour mantle

brighter than Joseph's fabled coat.

We stroll through October's perfume,

in the palm of a forest citadel,

embraced by the hush of leaves falling.

The burnt amber sky vibrates,

in ghostly whispers and sighs,

setting the table for twilight.

Nature nudges our hearts,

as we walk inside her harmony

through these October woods.

Blackbirds

A congregation of blackbirds

fidgets on the riverbank,

waiting for a crow ferry

to transmit them

to the far side of the moon.

Sonnet to Autumn

September is a time to start anew;
The heat of summer's gone and nights are cool,
When even those retired find much to do,
While youth of every age head off to school.

The season we call fall has been misnamed;
Throughout the land we rise from summer's rest.
The harvest sown in spring must be reclaimed,
With fields of wheat to stack and grapes to press.

November will bring frost to nip our feet;
By then we've shed the last of summer's tan.
Hoards of sweets are gone from trick or treat,
While Jingle Bells invite the jolly man.

When naming seasons only this I know:
The substance sure to fall is winter's snow.

Madeira Park Palette

(B.C. Sunshine Coast)

Rainbows glisten through sprinkler spray

on a golf-course lawn

ablaze in red carnations

pink petunias and blue lobelia

all blooming in the mist

On the front porch grandpa slumbers in his rocker

softly snoring in the morning sun

A Yellow Warbler greets me with her song

Bright flags flutter

reds and blues and white and gold

across a robin-egg sky

Navy-blue awnings flap

over milk-white boats

A fisherman in orange shirt

coils rope along the wharf

Two mighty eagles drift aloft

while crows and seagulls

chase and tease the pair

In the crystal dockside water

beneath the mossy bank

held firm by copper-skinned Arbutus

strands of bulb-kelp float like massive bullwhips

jellyfish flutter – translucent water butterflies

above brown-green crab

orange starfish rockfish and prawns

Kayak paddlers gracefully glide

A sailboat trails a yellow dingy

Two outboard motors growl

and a dog barks

Happy children play on the pier

On the hillside

in speckled sun among the ferns

I hear the forest breathing

while snow-capped mountains

slip into the sea

A Day Cruise on the Eagle

(B.C. Sunshine Coast)

From Egmont, cruising north, the inlet's calm
and we relax in sun and cooling breeze
to view the ponderous slopes with snowy peaks
and seals that raise their heads like massive slugs
on rocky islets, while we drift slowly by.

Black mussels and white-shelled oysters
mark the tides along the granite cliffs
where manganese leaches down
in white blotches.
And on a stretch of mossy shore,
age-stained boom-sticks stand forlorn in piles
to wait for harvests in another time

Beyond the Malibu Rapids,
Mt. Albert casts his head above the clouds.
Skidder trails zigzag down mountain slopes
in lighter green of alder amidst the pines,
like brush strokes of frustration
on a canvas of bright sun and darker hues.

Above Deserted Bay, fire-burned tips,
like silver spires, stand tall
among the virgin green of new-growth –
Western Hemlock and Red Cedar.

Princess Louisa Inlet

(B.C. Sunshine Coast)
shíshálh First Nations name "wiwelát"

When the Creator made swíwelát,
long before the mile-thick ice rolled down,
he thrust his mighty arms up through the mud
and flung the seed of forests to each side,
among the crags of granite and green stone.
No finger from the sky pronounced the deed,
though claps of thunder echoed hill to hill.
Then crowds of raven, crow and eagle came
to call the task well done and state their claim.

West Coast Morning

Dawn haze lifts from turquoise, beige,

radiant edifice – fifteen shades

green and blue;

smudge of robin's egg peeking through

to promise sun and maybe sprinkles

here and there;

a pleasant walk

or sea-wall cycle in between.

All about the city – cars, coach, sky-rail

wend their way to shop or school.

Motorists seldom blare or honk.

Lotusland a laid-back burg,

throngs moving, grooving,

happy purpose in their gait;

time to stop for early brew;

recyclers smile as they retrieve

their forenoon treasures.

West coast morning,

sweeping clean,

fulfilled.

Ocean Dock on Gambier Island

Crystal waters cold and clear
windows to a secret life
of shellfish – starfish –crab
Schools hopscotch over briny rocks
beneath urchin-hugged pier
Mist droplets sprinkle.
Fluttering breezes carry
fresh pine and iodine
to cleanse city lungs,
wash cluttered minds.
Yellow warblers' joyful tones
massage the ear

Vancouver

we cycle on paths where the grass is green
below snow - covered peaks in april sun
boats in the harbour, bobbing at anchor
ripple reflections of tall buildings
clean-vibrant-oriental-western
cherry blossomed avenues
dogwood daffodil
totems tulips
rhododendron
city in bloom
***
*

Cambie Bridge

Ben Nuttall-Smith
2003

Vancouver Early Morning

Soft haze on indigo mountains –
jagged teeth above tufts of steaming pine,
Last rays of full moon reflect on skyscrapers

columns of silver, light blue, pale green.
Cool breeze flutters red and white flags,
swallows chuckle the sleep-bound house

seagulls scream to rouse this city
as my family slumbers still.
Vancouver on a Sunday morning

City at Night

The city wears a different dress at night,
black gown with diamonds, emeralds, rubies
She sings a softer tune.

Her voice is muted yet a happier tone
than all the hustle of the daytime grind.
She's celebrating.

Granville Island
Reflection

Guitar picker crooning while

two deaf-mutes sign so loud

can't hear the words he's sobbing

into the wobbly microphone

under the red awning

on a lazy Granville Island

summer afternoon

Tiny tot, tied to his nanny

by a loving eye

teases pigeons while

midday shoppers hunt for parking spots and

long-haired daddy in sandals and shorts

dripping ice cream cone in one hand,

pushes a stroller with the other.

Give the man a loonie for his song

about tear drops and long lonesome nights.

MEMORIES

Childhood
Memories

– England

Lullabies, horsey rides, stories read from books,
plasticine, song time, picnics in the woods,
Punch and Judy, dressing up, swinging on the gate,
blackberries,   stinging nettles. Wasps!

Peppermint, licorice, sparklers on the tree,
Oranges, fairy circles, first snow on the lawn,
Father Christmas, bunnies, and a Teddy bear for me.
green apples,   hairbrush, "Ow!"

Pencils, crayons, snuggling by the fire,
camp fires, sing-songs, swimming in the sea,
red boots, puddles, a fishing pole and hooks,
toy trains,   aeroplanes, "Bed!"

Lollypops, wishing wells, gypsies in a field,
elephants, monkey nuts, rolling down a hill,
bunny rabbits, crocodiles, ponies, and a deer,
road blocks,   air raids. Pow!

Car rides, rope swings, robins in a nest,
gas masks, blackouts, nights beneath the stairs,
pup tents, parachutes, soldiers in a ditch,
doodlebugs, buzz bomb, Dead!

Chelsea Terrors

In 1941, I left my teddy bear behind.
You smothered all my faerie dreams,
drowned my childhood
in Gold Leaf, London Dry,
and flickering silver screen promises.
You oozed over me,
an albuminous silver streak of spotted slug.
You immersed me in your cobwebs and sour sweat.
Night after night after night,
you drove your poison dart deep, deep, deep –
and no one heard my sobs.

Outside your lair,
the Chelsea world screamed another agony.
Before the moaning sirens ceased,
the shrieking metal fell.
it filled the crumbling streets with flames –
and running,
                running,
                    running.

No place was safe
to hide away.

Wartime Crossing

British youngsters Liverpool to Halifax,

March, 1945

Lifeboats deck level ready,
hiding place for hidden pleasures,
pilfered Sweet Caps and Spearmint gum,
beneath the canvas, hid from adult eyes

We'd have our ears boxed, backsides booted,
depending on who caught us, if they did.

Played our dreams of Indians and birch canoes,
skis and all we'd heard from men on board
of miles and miles of prairie wheat,
cowboys, horseback Mounties, bears, wolves,
and mountains even taller than the Alps.
Enthralled, we did not hear the call to "action stations".

We were used to bombs and guns,
played bravado and were thrilled in our excited fear.
Then the hoot of ships' horns, running boots
and the thump-thump of depth charge "ash cans",
dropped to kill Donitz's boys,
slinking beneath the waves.

Peeking out we watched the flash and smoke
of battle on the frothy sea
and fired our finger guns
at submarines we could not see.
Nor could we stop to pick up sailors
screaming in the icy waves but plowed through
oil-soaked men who cursed us as they drowned.

When all was calm and we snuck out,
and when frantic mothers boxed our ears,
we said not where we'd been, nor what we'd seen.
Yet in restless sleep for nights and years to come
we'd shrink from blood-soaked hands
and see the scattered flames that brought them death.

Hitchhiking Over Christmas

New Brunswick, December 1950

I stood, lonely,
shivering, a solo leaf about to fall.
Night swatted away the sun,
sewing up the last rays of evening.

A great white silence
cracked cheeks and eardrums.
Winter wind with razor teeth
flayed my flesh and split my lips.

Snow and ice crawled through my veins.
Tears froze to my cheeks.
I heard the uncanny yowls
of wolves at the forest edge.

I moved stamping,
silky squeak of snow underfoot.
Nearby, a stream yattered, a forsaken gossip,
a guard dog muttered disheartened warnings.

In the distance, children chanted carols.
At home, women would be stuffing turkeys
baking tortière in cozy kitchens,
stockings hanging by the fire.

Alzheimer
Reflections

Mother painted nymphs in the woods
free as Chagall's women floating over houses,
her own spirit freed by dementia
danced in childhood innocence

nurses confiscated paint and brushes
to prevent splattered bedding.
she soiled sheets anyway,
laughed at the irony.

pale as butter, soft as peaches
a candle waiting for a match
memories wash up through fungicidal fog
like seepage on a stagnant beach

road map legs
hands hung limp as rope ends
she traced imaginary journeys
through varicose highways on her hands

she seemed embarrassed
merchandize fondled in a lingerie shop
her look softened – a lamp turned down
a carnival of bedclothes and jerseys

the week dragged on,
feet lugging the hours like convict chains
she chased her breath inside an oxygen mask
I run my memory along the razor's edge of those
last days

                         a drenching of regret

w i n t e r

this haunt of freshest nature
now so desolate since you and i here stood.
orchards and fields bewail their widow state,
stripped of their brood,

ah! what fond memories this spot brings back:,
glorious, intimate times:
your smiles,
your tears,
forgiveness for a lovers' spat.
two hearts content.

but, just as autumn's cold, cruel winds
strip gentle nature to the bone,
foul, furious death descends on epidemic's wings
to leave me here,
alone

Handyman's Delight

i chose to live high on that hill
above the ocean, in that tiny house
that needed so much care
top to bottom,
where rats sat glaring
from basement corners.
they ran across my bed at night
and tickled with their whiskers
while i tried in vain to sleep
to the cough and sputter and squeak
of the oil furnace reek,
while centipedes and spiders
crawled across my pillow in the dark.
smoky rays of morning sun
peeped through the rickety blind
that hung by a thread,
over the sliding glass doors
that led to the patio with cracked cement.
ants marched single file,
in snaking columns,
under the door to the Coca Cola can
that sat in front of the dusty brick fireplace
full of soggy newspapers
and rusty tins.
all that was far better
than natter, natter, natter.

T e r p s i c h o r e

last night,
Terpsichore,
my princess
fluttered white silk,
pulsed moonbeams,
incandescent
in her beauty.
her halo stayed my heart
and took away my breath.
we danced
in gentle rhythm,
father and daughter
in ritual parting.
a little girl,
bride to handsome consort.
a grown man,
tears in his eyes,
for the things
that won't come again.

g r a n d d a u g h t e r
a t
f o u r   m o n t h s

did your mother know how beautiful
you were floating like an astronaut
on your lifeline within her extended form
as she sang her starlit lullaby?

tiny hands flexed then
tiny legs pushed

now those same hands reach to grasp my fingers;
legs push down and lift you up
our eyes meet in wonder,
beaming, exalted at your accomplishment
both mouths open in delight.

TRAVEL

Manuela

(Buenos Aires)

Yesterday Manuella

at a café on Florida Street by Centro Pacifica

I sat at a sidewalk table

in the company of prosperous Porteños

and pampered tourists

I sipped Quilmes

and ate zucchini, fried greens

and filet mignon wrapped in bacon strips

You sat on the sidewalk too

around the corner at the curb

an angel with shabby wings

seven-year-old mother

to a baby brother

both unbathed

unschooled

unhoused

unfed

bed of dirt and rags beneath a leaky roof

What will become of you Manuella

as the tourists pass you by?

Who will love your baby brother?

How dare I ask when I eat so well in your city

around the corner from where you sit

silently pleading?

You are myriad Manuella

on the streets of Buenos Aires

in the subte

in the villas miserias

Last night you visited me in a dream

I tried to help you

My stomach had turned to stone

Oaxaca Weaver

see her now
by pink adobe wall
beneath bougainvillea orange
knees sway on mat of faded reed
between column and loom
back straps taut
her small dark fingers flit
back - forth, back - forth
her shuttle glides
carded wool - purple, green
indigo tint of heaven
pale gold of sacred hummingbird
eagle wing
breeze of eternity
scattering of stars
teardrops of the moon
robozo for a new mother

Sunset Shift at Café de Flores

Sunset flashes green on the purple sky

amidst orange, yellow, and golden clouds.

A kite glides the thermals;

swallows skitter, chasing gnats.

While strumming a twangy-mellow tune,

a guitarist speaks softly to us.

Tables are spread in Mexican array:

flickering candles, brilliant colours.

Suddenly the sky darkens.

Traffic and blaring megaphones overwhelm.

Here on the cafe rooftop,

life's cacophony dominates the night.

Quétzalcoatl

at Cholula, beyond the smoking mountains,
you sat in sacred effigy,
with your yellow face,
red beak,
feather mantle, red, white, black,
butterfly jewel,
diadem crown.
and on your feet,
gold socks,
golden sandals.
Quet-zal-coatl.
to you, mighty wind god,
we gave our fairest youth.
in forty days of feast and birdlike dance,
he honoured you
and then, upon your holy altar,
we gave you his heart.
his flesh became your flesh.
in sacred union,
we ate your body
and drank your blood.
you died by proxy
and rose again.
in your rising,
we were born again.
but you despised our offering.
as you yourself had prophesied,
you returned,
as bearded warriors in gleaming helmets,
seeking gold.
then, in your fury, you made war
with mighty Tez-cat-lipoca,

Smoking Mirror,
king of gods,
and with Vit-zil-op-ochli,
the Humming Bird, the mighty war god.

daily, we offered many hearts
of youths and slaves and captive warriors
to hurry Smoking Mirror
in your defeat.
with fiery thunder-sticks
you smashed our altars,
threw down our gods,
laid waste our cities of stone,
and burned our sacred books.
you planted foreign gods
in dome-topped temples.
while waging lesser wars,
Smoking Mirror swore revenge.
four hundred years flew by.
humming bird rested.
emerging from the dust of pathways north,
the conquering helmets took new form
with foreign names:
Pontiac, Buick, Ford.
Humming Bird, disguised as one of them,
found shapes to vent his anger.
once more the dismal drum of bold Hui-chil-o-bos
shakes the hills
with sound of conch and blaring horns.
the silver helmets roar and grind and screech
in mighty battle.
all around, with acrid smoke,
Mexico's blood spills out
and roadside shrines
mark the place of sacrifice.

Ode to the Cementerio Recoleta

(Buenos Aires)

Feral cats patrol avenues and narrow lanes

of crumbling mausoleums.

Magnificent gloss-black tombs

hold faded caskets

with rusted handles,

cracked plaster,

shattered stained glass.

Wealthy corpses moulder in dust

of wilted flowers

and broken vases.

Rats and birds crap just as freely

on rich and poor.

When I die, build me a hostel

for orphans,

urchins,

homeless waifs.

Do not write my eulogy in stone

but on the hearts and lips

of children not yet born.

Cast my ashes to the wind;

I'd not be happy here.

Señora de la gota
— Bead Lady
(Mexico)

Weighed down with bags of beads,
hand-crafted rosaries, shell crucifixes,
trays of bracelets, necklaces, and earrings,
a colourful pedlar walks the strip.
Today, as every day, she approaches me,
insistent I see her wares.
I shake my head, "Non, gracias."
She persists. At last, I give in.
A set of tiny pearls catches my fancy.
I pay a sum, tiny for me, a day's wages for her.
Like crumbs dropped for hungry gulls, I'm marked.
Now, up and down the glistening mica beach,
every pedlar wants his share.
Husband, wife, father, mother, son, and daughter,
all lug their wares.
Before the sun-blaze on the sand,
the poor families walk in silhouette.
The children jump the waves, shriek to catch up.
All head for me.

Ben Nuttall-Smith
Oaxaca, Mexico, 2004

A Portrait

Unpainted

– Naoussa, Paros

Were I to paint the scene from here,
beneath the tamarisk trees,
I'd pick a bright palette
and let the colours run.
For upper sky, cerulean,
violet for the bay:
with touches of cobalt,
turquoise and ultramarine.
Then for the rocks and sand,
I'd choose a wash of sparkling grey,
light ochre, burnt sienna
patched with olive, sap green, and sun
to keep the picture warm.
In the light and pleasant breeze,
I'd trim the whitewashed houses
all in bird's egg blue,
with rows and rows of olive trees.
Yet, could I paint the joyful sounds
of singing birds, music,
laughter and children on the beach,
and tinkling waves upon the shore?
How could I paint
the perfumed mix
of salt and fish
and sunscreen on my nose?

Cadgwith Fog

Swallows and gulls swoop, twirl, and glide

through fields of thick white mist,

myriad players in a sky ball game.

Beneath the field, framed in mottled green,

stand cottage roofs of slate and thatch.

a lonely spire invokes the sun,

to break the seal of fog

and post the winning score.

Footpaths to the Sea

with aching limbs and gnarled, knobby cane

the old man puffs, pants to keep astride

his youthful companions cantering down

the winding footpath to the sea.

he arrives, he sits, his gasping abates.

children race, shout with joy to reach the cove;

chase gulls, from congregation on the slip

of splintered shell among the frothy weed,

to frantic flight.

the old man sits, watches, remembers.

a tear slides down his cheek.

Galway Roads

beech trees
overhang sun-mottled puddles
glistening
from the night's rain
blackthorn
fringes line high hedges
freckled
with white wild garlic and bluebells
hairpin turns
spring upon narrow stone bridges
sometimes we stop and turn back
sometimes they do
sign at blind corner
free range children
careful

My Heart is Full

Hulls of orange, purple, banana yellow, lime green.

striped sails billowing and pulling, the sailboats glide,

like quetzal feathers on aquamarine.

Frothy white sparkles splash my feet.

My love emerges from the water, dripping, sun-kissed,

with her shell earrings, necklace of snowy pearl, and emerald swim dress.

Silver hair glistening in the morning sun,

warmer than all the sand and sea, she smiles.

Sugar Time

In the springtime, when the thaw winds
Bring the sugar farmer home,
I will hurry to the bushland,
Near my place by Saint Jerome

Light the fires and scrub the cauldrons.
Tap the maples' steady flow.
Busy friends have time to join me,
Making taffy in the snow.

Sonnet to Travel

Each time I pack my bags to go abroad,
All seven pairs of socks are picked with care.
My six best shirts, all ironed and neatly stored,
With handkerchiefs, and matching underwear.

I always bring two jerseys, one a spare.
Sometimes those tropic nights can turn quite cool.
And naturally, I'll take my favourite pair
Of jackets, without which I'd look the fool.

For formal evenings, tuxes are the rule.
We ought to be prepared to dine and dance.
My swimming trunks, for lounging by the pool
And, goodness me, let's not forget my pants.

Our destination's picked, we've spared no cost,
We pray this time our bags will not get lost.

ON THE

DOWN SIDE

Homeless

She spends her days
curled up on tattered rags
and soggy cardboard mats,
in crooked doorways
and by graffiti marked dumpsters,
on the cold hard sidewalk,
drowning slowly in the unforgiving rain.
When she's hungry
she roots for scraps of second hand, spoiled food,
behind greasy spoons and burger joints,
dining in bleak alleys on dark side of skid row.
Should she chance to find a half-inch butt
that's not been crushed,
she'll cadge a light,
remembering when she smoked a pack a day.
Those days long gone now,
just a hazy memory.
Once, she went to work each morning,
drove her kids to daycare and school.
For nineteen years she worked;
then, one day, she walked away.
No one knew where she'd gone
or why.
Now here she is,
a broken down angel,
a tarnished woman
wrapped in tattered rags
and shattered dreams.
With fixed stares,
we all hurry by her.
We don't even want to know her name.

Friday's Corner

whiskey stares on Friday's corner
in polluted stupor
purrs her way along East Hastings

like a dream, pissing in the wind
lives in a chemical straightjacket
carries courage in brown paper bag

at the Carnegie Library
"hanging" for a square meal
"Who's feeding that under-bitch?"

a congregation of women
squander words like summer rain
men spit Gatling expletives

in rounds of rapid fire
preacher, pits and crater face,
revels in fermentation and fornication

crab apple eyes and blackthorn tongue
sullen as Scottish Sunday
delivers his holy harangue

old geezer, carnivorous gaze
silver hair – outstretched wings of snowy owl
eyes – aluminum ball-bearings

toothless oyster
hands cracked and calloused
barnacles on Newfoundland dory

a drunk waiting to happen
throws epithets
at the oppressive pulpit

flings the universal sign
of disapproval
curses the zero God

Slum landlord
stomach preceding him
clutches stuffed wallet

F i x

I've tasted hatred at your reeking
alcohol-tobacco breath,
rough hands prying and taking.
cockroach crawling room, stained walls,
newspaper-pasted windows,
despair and sweat.

nowhere to go.
cops just as soon bust me
as hear my moaning.
when you're down, you're down;
every pimp and bimbo has your number.
need another trick to get my fix.

In City Towers

From turrets of mortar, steel and glass,
in hypnotic trance, they grasp for Zion
a glimpse of Yahweh, if He be there.

Babylon screams her multi-tongued clamour
above the howl of musac grinding.
Each wretch enclosed in solitary shell

they ponder meaninglessness
amidst the city's frantic chatter
and signs of uncivilization.

While sun sears through the urban smog,

discarded sheets of violent news oppress
in oily grime by cracked sidewalk.

Here sits a ragged crone,
discarded parka, cardboard mat,
paper cup with fifty cents.

Far from the balm of tree and brook,
she's never known a cow or sheep
or savoured air of mountain mist.

Instead, she clutches plaintive sign
hand-writ by ballpoint pen:
"Aids – God bless".

Jimmy Paul

they was callin' guys up

i'm as good as the rest

i'm a Shíshálh

proud Canadian too

ready to fight for king and country

Red Ensign flag

my country

my nation

so i go

wear the tartan

and the rifle

and march to sicily in worn-out boots

in germany

this kraut shoots through

my hand and

my arm

still got three good fingers

still can shoot a rifle

and lift a pint

or two

or three

but

i can't lift a pint

when i ain't allowed in

then they kick me off the reserve

and say

you not status indian

an' people look at me and say

hey, Jimmy Paul, where the hell ya bin

hell of a lot they know

government kept my pension too

most of it

hell, yes, i love my country

do it all again

god damn Ottawa

let me buy you a beer

this one's on me

the old man

clatter! bing! bang! boom!

spring pounds on city sidewalks

skateboards scrape

hot tires squeal

shouts and laughter echo off the buildings

basketballs bound on post and fence

and dribble past and back and 'round the old man

lost

in his past

clatter! bing! bang! boom!

battle screams in the night sky

engines roar

ack-acks pound

shouts and curses fearfully sound

big bombs whistle as the walls resound

shrapnel whines past his head

MIRACLES

he reached out with tattooed hand
and healed
I saw it with tear-filled eye
two shattered, lonely lives
became one

she took that rugged palm
crushed it with one tear
I saw it melt - I watched him melt
every day
miracles.

SPIRITUAL

Symphony of Life

What magic wonder sparkles

in the eyes of a child

discovering life in glittering sand

beside a frothy sea

Tiny creatures in the foam

hold their breath marveling

at what they too might well become

a trillion years from now

The child knows and gently holds

primordial ancestor

then puts her back

into the brine

to play another note

in the symphony of life

Ben Nuttall-Smith 2007

Beginnings

Further than a thought I flit,

beyond a trillion sparks of dust,

past worlds of ice and fire and blood.

A moth far fled from space and time,

my nakedness adorned with shooting stars.

What is a single day, when all has come from nothing,

in the flash of thought and Word?

An immeasurable spiral of unimaginable beauty.

All the years, as far as dreams can reach, are nothing

in the emptiness of space and time.

This was but the first day.

Hummingbird

hummingbird died in my hand
mistook rippled reflections on patio door
for brilliant blue of sky

I picked her up, tiny heart beating
faster than the midnight freight
pounds beneath my window

she blinked her tiny eyes
sighed farewell
is there a hummingbird heaven

or will she return to fly again
a hummingbird reincarnation?
How does the nestling,

born on a Oaxaca hill,
know the nest woven here
in our arbutus?

same bird as last year but younger still
a creature so minuscule
yet mighty enough to merit Toltec worship.

b i r t h   s o n g

when i was a tiny speck
in my mother's womb
right beneath her beating heart
the jungle drummed

she retched each morning
cursed me
loved me
sang to me
savage lullabies

i heard the loud duet
of the megapodes
calling kee-keer-kew
and learned to sing
my baby song

for good measure
i kicked
just to say
love you, mom

My World

i want to grow up in a world
where little birds nest in the trees,
i want to feel the breeze
taste the cool clean air
i want to walk down by the river,
see the moon among the ripples,
count the stars and smell wild flowers
and know I'm free.

all my neighbours would be friendly;
they'd be white and brown and black.
and i'd know each name
and show them that i care.
i want my children to be happy,
and my children's children too.
i need to know they'll laugh and sing
and cry like me.

in that world we'd fight all wars
around a table in a hall
with wooden soldiers and lead sailors
in a line
and the losers and the winners
would invite us all to dinners
where we'd cheer the referee,
a child of nine.

what a world this world would be
where i'd need you and you'd need me
and every one we met would smile
and call us "friend".

if we hurry, we might make it,
change the world before they break it.
call for love
and bring the madness to an end.

Creation

Mother Earth

from your womb

the ocean

you give birth

we are of your substance

Ammonia, Methane, Hydrogen, Helium,

created in the nuclear furnaces of stars,

stirred by sun's heat

volcanic eruptions

lightening

RNA, DNA

multiplying

expelling oxygen

producing Carbon,

calcium, phosphorus

Nature

complicity

intricacy

mystery

rhythm

Life

I Am

spirit

I am spirit and water

I am spirit, water, carbon

sung in the light of tears

living countless memories

dreams, memories, hopes, regrets choruses in my head

forever now

somewhere

in the infinity of space

I am stardust

wrapped in the cool grey fog of time

beyond all concepts

beyond thinking

God and the hereafter

grandparents of the unborn

We are all grandparents of the unborn

listening to anonymous voices

one informs, the other reminds us

of what we have chosen to forget

sprayed with pesticides and ethicides

in the pursuit of profit

walls

feuds and revenge

flies and runny noses

assassination, execution, martyrdom –

take your choice

as for me,

I'll go out

riding a unicorn

with a song

a s o n n e t t o
s t a r d u s t

"N o l i t e T i m e r e"

This story has many beginnings.
It's the ending that's elusive.

An old man shakes off his city clothes –
Trilby hat in brown plaid,
knee length Burberry,
gray silk cravat,
blue dress shirt with fraying cuffs,

black braided belt, silver buckle,
alligator moc toe shoes flecked with mud,
stained white over-the-calf socks, garters,
form-fitting riding breeches,
and tattered long-johns.
He drops a boar skin wallet, Gucci watch,
Sony Ericsson cell phone
and an assorted set of keys on a ring
into a large bin labeled "recycling".
Then, from a long rack, he selects
a rough woolen robe.
Thus garbed, and with cold bare feet,
he walks into the night.

Once upon a lifetime,
eons ago, and far into the future,
as suns blaze then sink into silent black holes.
As other universes sizzle into being,
a monk, servant to a timeless Father God
or Mother Goddess,
lives alone on a great arid plain.

One long and dusty day,
when the biting winds chew at his blistered nose
and bluebottle flies sting his festering cheeks,
the monk feels his end draw near
and journeys out into the desert.
He sits in the cooling sand.
He gazes at the immensity of stars.
In these times, they sparkle brilliantly,
even in the noon day sun.
The swirling galaxies swarm in the purple sky
as if some astronomical charwoman
has shaken out her dust mop in the great wind.

I know this is true.
I am that lonely monk.
I am old and my joints ache, even in the dry air.
I lift my withered arms high up;
the stars envelop me.
I float like a wafted dry leaf,
up inside the Milky Way.
Down mega light years below,
I see the planet Earth.
Faster and faster,
it spins like a moth around its flickering candle star.
Soon it's a speck of sand
amid a trillion other worlds.

I watch the Earth I had known evaporate.
It is a dewdrop in the morning sun.
My hand is full of spinning orbs of brilliant light.
Meteors pierce my naked thigh.
Yet I feel no fear.

Long ago, my robe of wool and hemp
had floated from my limbs.

Suddenly, I feel a light too bright to bear.
At its centre is a spinning, pulsating sphere.
Sometimes the circle is a great triangle.
Other times, it's a tiny baby.
From the light comes a great wind,
blowing in steadily increasing circles.
Shhhhpheeeeuuuw!

I float inside an enormous, living heart.
I hear the steady rhythm.
"Badoom! Badoom! Badoom!"
A timeless voice calls out to me.

At first, it's loud. Then it's soft.
Next it's a whisper, like a breeze in tall pines.
Then I hear an echoing tongue.
I don't recognize that Voice.
Yet I embrace its invading message:
"Ego sum, nolite timere."

It is I. Fear not.

Crusaders of the New Tomorrow

Jackboots crash on cobble highways,
gentle byways. Where pilgrim, knight,
and merchant soles once softly swept,
and high-stepping steeds pranced,
monster tanks flaunt and flare their cursed smoke
as they scratch and screech rumbling blasphemy.

Twisted crosses, black on red,
jigsaw across shields and pennants.
Ever flowing blood feeds fields of poppies,
acres of brilliant poppies,
worlds of poppies.
Who can staunch it?

In the woods, trees bend and break,
twisted, splintered, ruined.
and from heaven's realm, death-screaming eagles
fling down eggs of destruction.
Cathedrals, castles, mansions, hovels, entire cities
are only smoldering memories.

Moaning shells, pale yellow-green gas,
slowly burning corpses piled helter-skelter:
Dogs sniff about, quarrel in the stench.
The torn ones, young and old, moan unconsoled
while mothers clutch wailing infants and weep.
Others stagger about, helpless.

In this rubble of hatred, death, and curses,
a tiny blossom pushes through the toxic dust,
mute promise of a new day

POETRY

AND

READING

The Public
Library

The public library is the great equalizer.
Young and old, rich or poor, scholar or ignoramus,
all are welcome without charge.

Enter without restriction.
Drink in the knowledge of the ages.
Take up a book, any book.

Feast your eyes and your mind
on the learning of the ages.
Travel to the inaccessible corners of the Globe.

Need a question answered?
Looking for a recipe?
Ask a librarian.

Sumerians, Greeks, Romans, all had libraries.
Toltec, Mayan and Aztec had their books.
Ignorant men destroyed them.

Public Libraries and Public Schools have offered
learning to all since the mid Nineteenth Century.
Only fanatics and tyrants privatize or close libraries.

The Poem

Where will you go when this poem's done?
I'd like to join those of my persuasion
sighing contentment on library shelves
where books read themselves between the covers.

Some share dreams with romantic balladeers
while others grow sharp teeth,
hiss angry utterance at timid readers.
The page that holds these words was once a tree